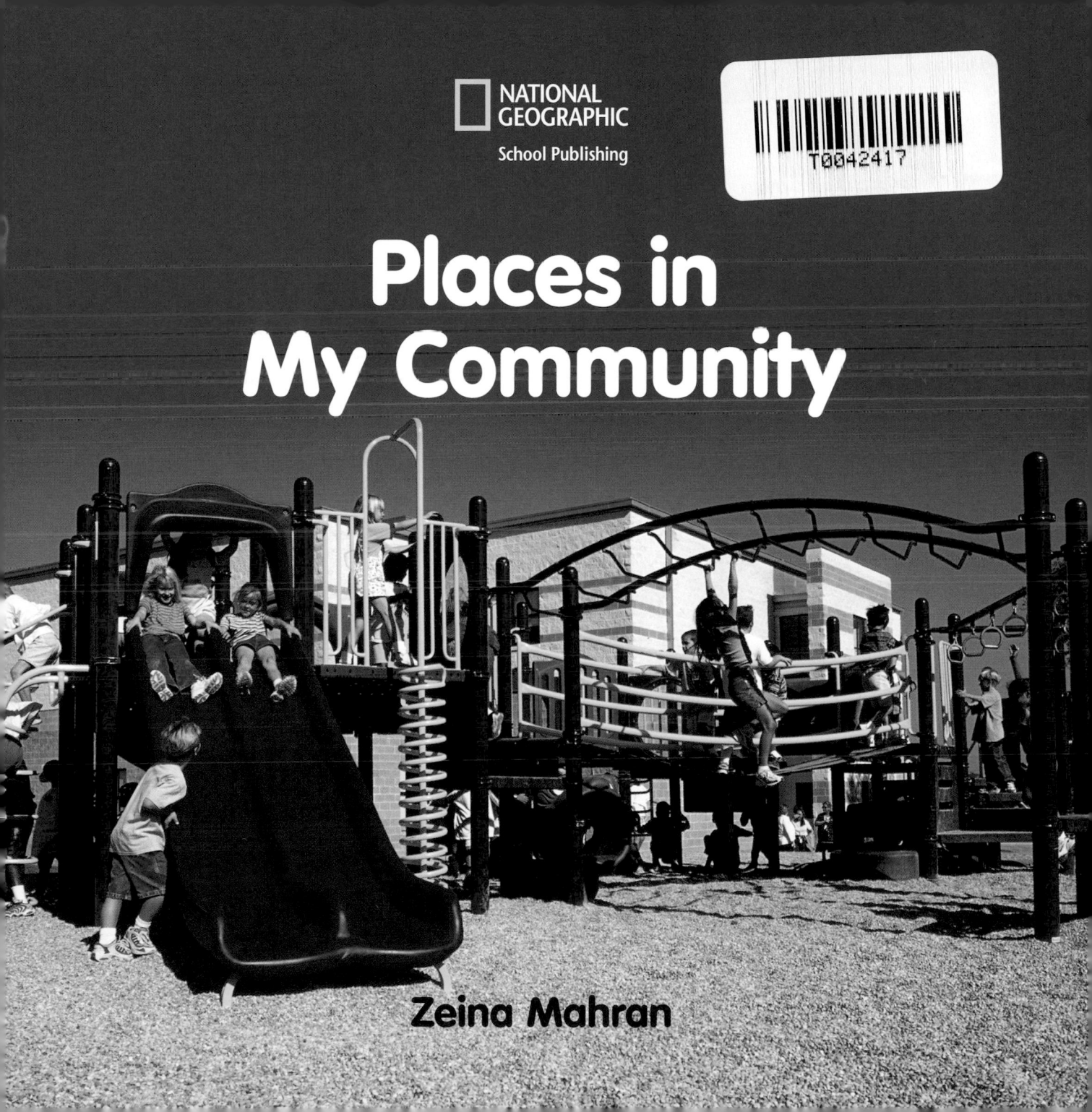
NATIONAL
GEOGRAPHIC
School Publishing
T0042417
Places in
My Community
Zeina Mahran

PICTURE CREDITS
Illustration by Roberto Fino (4–5).
Cover, 9 (above), 12, 16 (center left), Bill Aron/PhotoEdit, Inc.; 1, 4 (all), 5 (left), 7 (all), 8 (all), 11 (left), 14 (below left & above left), 16 (above right, center right, below left & below right), Photolibrary.com; 2, 6, 11 (above), 16 (above left), APL/Corbis; 5 (right), 11 (below right), Michael Newman/PhotoEdit, Inc.; 9 (below), 10, 13 (below left), 14 (right), Getty Images; 13 (above right), Mary Kate Denny/PhotoEdit, Inc.; 15 (above), Steve Skjold/PhotoEdit, Inc.; 15 (below) Jeff Greenburg/PhotoEdit, Inc.

Produced through the worldwide resources of the National Geographic Society, John M. Fahey, Jr., President and Chief Executive Officer; Gilbert M. Grosvenor, Chairman of the Board; Nina D. Hoffman, Executive Vice President and President, Books and Education Publishing Group.

PREPARED BY NATIONAL GEOGRAPHIC SCHOOL PUBLISHING
Ericka Markman, Senior Vice President and President Children's Books and Education Publishing Group; Steve Mico, Senior Vice President and Publisher; Marianne Hiland, Editorial Director; Lynnette Brent, Executive Editor; Michael Murphy and Barbara Wood, Senior Editors; Bea Jackson, Design Director; David Dumo, Art Director; Margaret Sidlowsky, Illustrations Director; Matt Wascavage, Manager of Publishing Services; Sean Philpotts, Production Manager.

MANUFACTURING AND QUALITY MANAGEMENT
Christopher A. Liedel, Chief Financial Officer; Phillip L. Schlosser, Director; Clifton M. Brown III, Manager.

BOOK DEVELOPMENT
Ibis for Kids Australia Pty Limited.

Copyright © 2006 National Geographic Society. All rights reserved. Reproduction of the whole or any part of the contents without written permission from the publisher is prohibited. National Geographic, National Geographic *Windows on Literacy*, and the Yellow Border are registered trademarks of the National Geographic Society.

Published by the National Geographic Society
1145 17th Street, N.W.
Washington, D.C. 20036-4688

ISBN: 0-7922-6053-8

Fifth Printing June 2018
Printed in the United States of America

Contents

Think and Discuss	4
Places to Live	6
Places to Work	8
Places to Shop	9
Places to Learn	10
Places to Play	11
Places to Do Things Together	12
Use What You Learned	14
Picture Glossary	16

Think and Discuss

Look at the places in this community.
Where do people live, work, shop, learn, and play?

Places to Live

A community has places where people live.

houses
mobile homes

Places to Work

A community has places where people work.

fire station

restaurant

Places to Shop

A community has places where people shop.

Places to Learn

A community has places where people learn.

Places to Play

A community has places where people play.

Places to Do Things Together

A community has places where people do things together!

community garden

neighborhood art project
swimming pool
community festival

Use What You Learned

A community has many different kinds of places. What places are in your community?

community

house

live

park

play

school

shop

store

Picture Glossary

house

library

playground

school

store